I0617316

Fun Bird Facts for Kids

Jacquelyn Elnor Johnson

www.CrimsonHillBooks.com

First edition, May 2022.

Cataloguing in Publication Data

Johnson, Jacquelyn Elnor

Fun Bird Facts for Kids

Description: Crimson Hill Books trade paperback edition | Nova Scotia, Canada

ISBN:	978-1-990887-03-1 (Paperback - Ingram)
BISAC:	JNF003030 Juvenile Nonfiction: Animals - Birds JNF016000 Juvenile Nonfiction: Curiosities & Wonders JNF048000 Juvenile Nonfiction: Reference - General
THEMA:	WNCB - Wildlife - Birds and birdwatching - General interest YNG - Children's - Teenage general interest - General knowledge and interesting facts YNNK - Children's - Teenage general interest - Birds

Record available at https://www.bac-lac.gc.ca/eng/Pages/home.aspx

Book design: Jesse Johnson

Crimson Hill Books
(a division of)
Crimson Hill Products Inc.
Lawrencetown, Nova Scotia
Canada

Crimson Hill
Books

A beautiful swan in a lake.

This is an adult Puffin. They summer on the shore, but spend their winters out at sea catching fish. Puffin chicks are called Pufflings.

Do you know birds?

Look up! Can you see them?

Listen! Can you hear them?

They're birds, and they live among us. There are 18,000 known species of birds alive today. They live everywhere humans live. They're so familiar we think we know them very well.

We like them for their songs, their bright colors and their cheerful signal that Spring is returning at last.

We admire their incredible diversity. We are amused by their cleverness. We're impressed by their astonishing hunting, flying, and diving abilities.

Birds entertain and inspire us, in our stories, poetry, art and music.

Even though they are a very different animal than we are, there are ways that birds are very much like people. It could be that's another reason we're fascinated by them.

There's so much people have learned from birds. It is birds who first showed people that flight is possible. They challenge us to get out into nature and enjoy it. They help pollinate plants. And there are many more ways birds help humans and our planet and always have. Humans have been on earth for about six or seven million years. Birds have been here for more than 150 million years. There is no time in human history when there weren't birds in our lives. Almost no human who has ever lived did not know birds.

But how well do we know them?

This is how an artist thinks ancient bird Archeopteryx might have looked on a day like today, but millions of years ago.

The truth is even now, after being together for so long, birds have secrets. Though we've learned so much about them, there is still more to discover! That's what this book is about.

Are birds really dinosaurs?

Some scientists say that birds are living dinosaurs. This is true, if you think about birds starting out as a dino cousin but then getting a lot smaller, developing wings and learning to fly. There were also other changes on the journey from being a dinosaur-like creature to the birds we know today. These changes happened over a very long time.

The ancient ancestor of both birds and the monster meat-eating dinosaurs is a smaller, much earlier type of dinosaur called theropods. All the theropods lived on the ground. They had sharp teeth. They could run fast. The bird most like these theropods that still lives today is the ostrich.

Some of the smaller theropods had feathers, but they couldn't fly yet. Then some of these theropods decided to move up into the trees. Maybe it was safer there. Or they could find more food in the tree-tops. At first, all these almost-birds could do was glide between the trees. Gradually they got smaller and their bodies got lighter. Their front limbs got stronger. They learned to fly. This all started about 150 million years ago.

The earliest true bird that looked like a modern bird is called Archaeopteryx [say this: arch-ee-op-ter-icks]. Archaeopteryx was about as big as a modern raven. It had wings with flight feathers. Though in some ways it was like a modern bird, it was still a lot like a dinosaur, with small teeth, no beak and a long bony tail. It could fly. Its front legs were becoming even better wings, but they still had three fingers with claws on the ends of those front wings.

There's still a lot we don't know about Archaeopteryx. Only six of them as fossils have ever been found, all in Germany. Fossils are the bones of their bodies, changed into stone. There are probably more very early bird fossils elsewhere in the world just waiting to be found.

Bird Fun Fact:
A bird's bones weigh less than their feathers.

Hooked fliers

Ancient bird ancestors like Archeopteryx had claws on their wings. We don't know exactly how these claws were used, but there is a bird alive today who also has claws on their wings. These claws aren't used to catch their prey. Instead, the Young Hoatzins use their claws to help them walk on the floor of the Amazon rain forest where they live.

Are birds reptiles?

All the reptiles except birds are cold-blooded. This means they have no way to warm their bodies except to find a warm place in the sun. They also can't cool off their bodies, except by finding a cool place to hide in water or a cave, under rocks or underground. Lizards, turtles, alligators, crocodiles and snakes are all reptiles.

Birds are also classified as reptiles. Classified means grouped in with by scientists and researchers. All reptiles have scales, a backbone, breathe into lungs and most of them lay eggs instead of having live babies.

Birds are the only reptile that is warm-blooded like the mammals. Even so, crocodiles are the closest living relative to birds. Dinosaurs, crocodiles and birds had the same ancestor, a creature that lived around 250 million years ago. It was a small animal that walked on four feet. Scientists have named this very ancient ancestor Archosaur.

A male Ovenbird building the nest he hopes will Wow his sweetie.

Home sweet nest

All birds lay eggs. Most of them lay their eggs in nests.

Birds have lots of different ways of building nests. Some nests are in trees. Some are on the ground or even underground. These nests are made of all the building materials birds are able to find. This could be twigs, leaves, feathers, mosses, lichens or things humans have left where birds can find them like pieces of string or clothes dryer lint.

Male Ovenbirds are master nest builders. They use several different nest designs in their hopes of wowing a female Ovenbird to move right in. The male might build a clay dome or a stick nest or an underground nest with cleverly hidden tunnels as the doors to get in.

Once his creation is finished, he will invite an attractive female to stop over for a visit. Females have a look around and decide on a male's homebuilding skills. If she's not pleased, the male Ovenbird will destroy his nest and start over!

Upside-down nester

The African Palm Swift uses her own spit to glue some of her feathers to the underside of a palm leaf. Then she glues her two eggs to this upside-down nest. She uses her claws as hooks to cling upside-down to this nest and keep her eggs warm. She adds to her nest later, so the chicks don't fall out.

The sewing bird

The Tailorbird is a songbird that lives in tropical parts of Asia. Tailorbirds use their beaks to cut holes along the edges of two leaves. Then they use pieces of grass to sew the two leaves together, creating a little leaf cave for their nest.

The prisoner bird

Female Great Indian Hornbills put themselves in prison with their nests! When she is ready to lay her eggs, a Great Indian Hornbill finds a hole in a tree she likes. Her mate seals up the hole, leaving just a tiny opening so he can shove in some food.

She lays her eggs and stays in her tree nest prison with them until the chicks are a few months old. Then, she breaks free and both parents hunt for food for their noisy growing family.

Bird hotels

The Hammerkopf is a wading bird that lives in parts of Africa and Madagascar. It builds the largest and strangest nest in the entire bird world. A Hammerkopf nest can be six feet or almost two metres high and just as big across. Their nest can weigh as much as 110 pounds, or 50 kilograms. This huge nest might be on the ground, but Hammerkopfs also like to build their nests in trees.

Because it is so large, it can take a Hammerkopf six weeks to build their nest. And there is so much room in and around this nest, other birds turn it into a nest hotel. Weaver birds, mynas and pigeons all like to attach their own nests to a Hammerkopf nest.

Another bird that prefers to live close to neighbours is the Sociable Weaver bird of South Africa. They get together to build huge bird hotels where as many as 100 bird families raise their young. Their nest hotels look like a huge haystack stuck in a thorny tree.

Bird Fun Fact:

The bird that has the longest feathers is the Onagadori. Their tail feathers can be almost 35 feet or 10.5 metres long!

The Peregrine Falcon, or Duck Hawk, is a powerful flier.

Nest protectors

All birds must protect their eggs and young from predators. Some birds have found a way to get animal friends to help them do this.

In Siberia, the coldest part of Russia, Red Breasted Geese are preyed upon by Arctic foxes. But the foxes are usually defeated by Peregrine Falcons who also share their tundra homeland. Peregrine Falcons are much smaller than the foxes, but also fiercer.

Red Breasted Geese build their nests around the Peregrine Falcons' nests for protection. In return, the Geese honk loudly when they sense a nearby fox, alerting the Peregrine Falcons who take to the air for swooping and vicious attacks on the foxes.

Bird Fun Fact:

African Gray Parrots have incredible memories. They can learn as many as 800 words or short sentences!

Insect guards

Most humans would rather not live close to wasps, but that's not true for Rufous Naped Wrens. They let the wasps serve as their bodyguards.

A different bird with a name that sounds almost the same, the Rufous Woodpecker, builds their nests in the middle of ant hills. The ants aren't pleased, but they soon get over being upset and instead they try to attack any other creature that tries to steal the Rufous Woodpecker's eggs.

Bad parent birds

Some birds would just rather not be parents at all. They lay their eggs in other birds' nests, leaving all the parenting work up to the unsuspecting foster parents.

The female Cuckoo is a master at this. She finds a likely nest belonging to a bird that is a different species. She carefully takes one egg out the nest, lays an egg of her own in its place and flies away. She usually takes the egg she has stolen from that nest. She is sly and quick. All this takes only about 10 seconds.

Cuckoo females are able to change the look of their own eggs to be just like the ones of the bird that owns the nest. No one knows how Cuckoos are able to do this mean but clever trick.

Some birds are smart enough to recognize eggs that aren't their own. They throw the 'wrong' eggs out of

This tiny European Robin has to work hard to feed the Common Cuckoo chick that was born in her nest.

their nests. Or they just abandon the nest and build another one for their own babies.

Cuckoos know about this. They are always trying to make their eggs look even more like the eggs of the birds Cuckoos choose to leave their eggs with. At the same time, those birds are always trying to find ways to discover which eggs or which chicks aren't their own.

Screaming Cowbirds only lay their eggs in the nests built by Bay-Winged Cowbirds. The Screaming Cowbird chicks look exactly like Bay-Winged Cowbird chicks. That is, until they leave the nest, when their feather colours change to look like their true, but very bad, parents.

A mother swan and her babies. They're called cygnets. Swans are good-parent birds, fiercely protecting their young.

Egg messages

American White Pelican chicks can tell their parents exactly what they want even before they hatch! While they're still inside their eggs, these babies can tell their parents when they're too hot or too cold. They do this by making loud distress calls their parents can hear. Then the parents rearrange the eggs to let them cool, or sit on them to warm them up.

Are birds like humans?

Birds are more like reptiles than they are like us. Even so, there are some important ways that birds are just like us.

Both birds and humans are warm-blooded. This means we can warm our bodies up, or cool them down, whenever we need to. The cold-blooded animals, including all the reptiles except birds, can't do this.

Another way birds and humans are alike is we are both vertebrates. This means we have a bone skeleton, including a spine, or backbone. All mammals and all reptiles also have a backbone.

Birds' bodies work something like human bodies do. One difference is that birds' hearts are beating faster than ours. They have a faster metabolism, which means their bodies are working faster.

Birds move faster and react faster than we can. To them, we must appear to be large, very slow-moving creatures. To us, they can move so fast that we don't quite see what they're doing or how they're doing it.

Their normal body temperature is also warmer than human body temperature:

Normal body temperature for humans is 98.6 degrees F. or 37 degrees C.

Normal body temperature for birds is between 102 to 109 degrees F. or 39 to 43 degrees C.

Birds just run hotter and faster than we do. One price they pay for their quick metabolism is almost all birds have much shorter lives than most people do.

Bird Fun Fact:

Birds walk on their toes. Other toe walkers are horses and all the members of the cat family including lions, tigers and pet cats.

This is a model of what a Pterosaur might have looked like.

Why birds can fly, but humans can't

Birds had to change in many ways to be able to fly. Their front legs, over millions of years, became wings. They developed more air sacks in their bodies to supply their wing muscles with extra oxygen to power their muscles. Their bones became very light, unlike human bones or the bones of other mammals. They also had to develop flight feathers.

People can't fly because we have bones that are filled with marrow, while birds' bones are almost hollow. Humans have no wings, and only two air sacks (our lungs) to take in air to get oxygen. We developed over millions of years to be land creatures. Like the birds

King Penguins are very good at living in very cold places. There are about 4.5 million King Penguins in the world today.

that can't fly and don't swim, humans developed to be best at running.

Did birds teach humans to fly?

The very first ancient animals who learned to fly, not just glide, where the pterosaurs, a flying reptile.

The largest bird that has ever existed was a pterosaur. It had a wingspan of 10 metres, or almost 33 feet! Not all the pterosaurs were so big. Scientists have found fossils of some as small as a modern sparrow.

Pterosaurs dominated the air from 150 million years ago until about 66 million years ago, when the dinosaurs died. This is called a Great Extinction Event, because all the dinosaurs died at about the same time. Scientists who study earth's animal history believe the reason the dinosaurs died is an asteroid hit Earth, causing earthquakes, volcanos to erupt and

This is an Emperor Penguin Dad and his chick. He's in charge while the baby's mother is out at sea, hunting for their dinner.

massive fires. Only the creatures that were small enough to find shelter in the water or underground, like crocodiles, insects, fish and ocean animals, the early mammals and early birds, survived.

Penguins used to fly

Once, penguin ancestors could fly like other birds, but they lost that ability millions of years ago.

All penguins are clumsy on land, but they seem to fly through the water, going as fast as 20 miles per hour, or 32 kilometres per hour. They need to be able to dive and swim quickly to get away from seals, their main predators.

When they lost the ability to fly, they developed heavier bones, to help them dive and hunt for fish underwater. Their wings also became more like little paddles so they could swim more quickly underwater. That's why they don't look like birds. Instead, they look like chubby torpedos with feathers.

Deep divers

Penguins are skilled divers, but they don't dive nearly as deep as Guillemots [say this: gilly-mots]. Guillemots look like little penguins, but they are actually shore birds who make their nests on rocky cliffs.

They can dive up to 150 metres, or almost 500 feet. The deepest underwater dive by a flying bird is 210 metres or 690 feet by a Brünnich's guillemot. They can also fly, up to 40 miles per hour or 64 kilometres per hour. Even in the bird world, it's unusual to be good at both flying and underwater diving.

Why don't penguins' feet freeze on the ice?

With their thick coat of waterproof feathers penguins standing on the ice can still stay comfortably warm. They also have a layer of fat under their skin for insulation from the frigid weather of Antarctica.

A Gentoo Penguin couple. Most penguins mate for life. This means they stay with the same partner to have their babies.

But their feet don't have feathers. So how do they keep their bare feet from freezing on the ice? When a penguin gets too warm, it can release the extra heat through its legs and feet. They can also change how much warm blood is travelling down their legs to their feet. This keeps their feet just warm enough to keep from freezing!

City penguins

A colony of little penguins have moved into a city in Australia. No one knows exactly why they did this. They started showing up about 30 years ago and now there are about 1,400 Fairy Penguins who live under St. Kilda Pier at Melborne Harbour.

Fairy Penguins are the smallest type of penguin. When they're swimming on the ocean, they look like shore birds. The adults are only about 12 inches or 25 to 30 centimetres tall.

If you ever visit Melbourne, you'll have to get up really early in the morning to see the Fairy Penguins. Around 5 a.m. they leave their nests under the pier to swim out to sea. They fish all day and return to their nests as the sun is setting.

They're graceful on the water and strong swimmers. On land, like all penguins, they're clumsy, walking and jumping to get back to their nesting places.

Their feathers change every year. At the end of October, which is Springtime in Australia, they get shiny new bright blue feathers. Gradually, their bright feathers turn a darker, duller blue until they moult, which means losing all the old feathers as the new ones grow in.

Fastest swimmers

In a bird underwater swimming contest, who'd take the Gold? The Gentoo penguin, whose home is Falkland Islands and Antarctica, would take the prize! They fly through the water at 22 miles per hour, or 36 kilometres per hour.

If there was a human competitor, they'd finish the race far behind the penguin. The fastest a person has

An Albatross looks awkward taking off and landing, but they are excellent fliers.

been clocked swimming underwater is only 6 miles per hour, or 9.6 kilometres per hour.

But if the world's fastest fish was in the contest, they'd easily win this race. The world's fastest fish is the Indo-Pacific Sailfish. They've been clocked racing through the ocean at 68 miles per hour, or 110 kilometres per hour.

Fastest Fliers

With a wingspan of 1 metre or 39 inches and eyesight eight times better than people have, the Peregrine Falcon is an impressive bird. They are able to see their prey up to 3 kilometres, or 1.8 miles away!

Peregrine Falcons are also the world's fastest bird flier, able to dive from the air while reaching airspeeds of up to 242 miles per hour, or 390 kilometres per hour.

Some Peregrine Falcons migrate from their summer breeding grounds on the tundra of the Arctic to their winter home in South America, an epic journey one-way of 15,500 miles or 24,945 kilometres.

Most Frequent Flier

Since birds learned to fly, they've developed some amazing flying feats!

A Pigeon can take off vertically. That means straight up in the air, like a helicopter.

An Albatross can travel as much as 62,140 miles, or 100,000 kilometres in a year. They can stay in the air for 9,320 miles, or 15,000 kilometres, before they need to land. They do this by locking their wings and gliding on the air currents so they don't get tired as quickly. Air currents are breezes or winds that are above the earth.

Centuries ago, sailors would spot Albatrosses flying far out to sea. They would point their ships in the direction the birds were flying, knowing that the birds were always flying towards land.

In 1887, sailors shipwrecked on the remote Crozet Islands in the southern Indian Ocean decided not to put a message in a bottle as their cry for rescue. Instead, they tied their message around the neck of an Albatross. Two weeks later, someone found that note on a beach in Australia that is 3,500 miles, or 5,600 kilometres away from where the sailors waited for help. All the shipwrecked sailors were rescued.

Are birds smart?

If someone called you a "bird-brain," you might be insulted. But actually, it's not an insult at all. Birds do have small heads, so there isn't a lot of space for their brains. But smaller doesn't mean dumber. Birds' brains, compared to the amount of space they take up in their heads, actually have more connections and can do more than human brains.

All birds are exactly as smart as they need to be to find clean water, healthy food and shelter and defend themselves from their enemies. Some birds have developed all this and are able to do some surprisingly smart things, like learn to sing new songs or mimic sounds they hear.

A Marsh Warbler can learn and remember 80 different songs!

The best talker among birds is the African Gray Parrot. They can learn the names of colors, shapes and things. They can count things and do simple adding questions like the ones kids do in Grade 2.

Crows can make simple tools to get food. They can also teach their chicks how to do what they can do.

Pigeons can always find their way home, even over long distances. Migrating birds always return each year to the same place where they were born.

Lorikeets are a Parrot that has a brush at the tips of their tongues to collect nectar. They're a smart and sweet-natured bird that can be a pet.

This Red Macaw is a Parrot. Parrots can live longer than any other bird. Some of them can get to be 120 years old!

Some birds can solve problems, count and remember where they put things. There's a lot more humans still don't know about how birds think and just how smart they really are.

Why aren't bats birds?

Like most birds, bats can fly. But bats aren't birds. They're mammals.

The reason is that bats have fur, not feathers. They don't lay eggs. Their babies are born live and get nutritious milk from their mothers as their first food. They also have a different way of flying than birds do.

Bats are the only mammal that can fly. They can fly really fast. In the air, they can reach speeds of more than 100 miles per hour, or 161 kilometres per hour. That's way beyond the speed limit in North America for cars and trucks on highways.

But even that great bat speed would lose against the world's fastest racing pigeons. They've been clocked at 110 miles per hour, or 177 kilometres per hour!

Parrots

Several birds have good memories. They return to the same places to nest each year. They remember good places to find food. Some are able to hear any sound and mimic it exactly.

But few birds have the ability to remember things for a very long time like parrots do. They only need to hear a word or a sound once to be able to make that sound for the rest of their lives.

Parrots are life-long learners. They can learn new things right up to the ends of their lives. Only some humans can do this.

Parrots might have heard a sound, just once, many years ago, but they can still repeat it. Why do they do this? It's probably just because they like the sound of what they're repeating, like the ping of a microwave or ringtone of a phone or a football chant they heard on TV. If you have a parrot, or want one, you might want to be really careful about what sounds you let your pet hear! They might be saying it, or singing it, for the rest of their very long lives!

Do birds like to dance?

It seems that some do. Cockatoos, a type of parrot, can dance to the beat of music they like. They can also work out some new moves, if they get the chance to hear different music that is faster or slower.

Why do they do it? No one knows. It isn't to attract a mate or get food or for any of the other reasons birds do things. Maybe they're just doing it for fun.

Only some types of parrots can all do this amazing happy feet feat. Songbirds can teach each other to sing. Scientists don't know yet if there are any birds who can teach each other to dance.

You can see some impressive bird moves if you go to Bird Singalong Project on Facebook. That's where pet owners are helping scientists study the amazing musical abilities of birds. There's even one bird that sings opera (and maybe some of the scientists can, too)!

Zebra finches

Every young male zebra finch chick listens to his father's song. That's how he first begins to learn to sing. Young males listen to their dad and all the neighbor dads and finally try singing themselves. At first, they're not very good, but they keep practicing. As adults, they'll sing their song to attract a mate.

Female zebra finches are impressed by the clearest and brightest courtship songs. Courtship is like dating.

Even after they have a family, the males will continue to sing their song, drawing their mate closer to them and then teaching their own children to sing. When males are just singing to themselves, the song might be kind of sloppy. Maybe a bit out of tune. They save the best performances of their lives for courtship.

The bird that can't run

Secretary Birds have long legs, so they look like they'd be good runners. Not true. They can't run at all. They can't even walk. Instead, they hop along, searching for lizards and snakes to eat in their home on the scrublands of Africa.

The bird that takes off backwards

The Quetzal can fly, but they have a strange way of taking off. They launch themselves off of branches backwards, something like a person with a parachute falling backwards out of a plane.

The reason for this strange take-off is that Quetzals have a tail problem. Their tails are so long that if they took off like other birds do, they could shred their very long tails. A Quetzal bird's tail is 3 feet, or a metre long! They nest in hollow trees, but have to back into their nests and curl their magnificent tails over their heads and out the tree hole. If you are in Central America and you spot some colourful feathers hanging on a tree trunk, it could be you've spotted a Quetzal in her nest with her tail parked outside.

A male Bower Bird creates his nest. Bower Birds search for objects to charm the one they want to mate with.

The decorator bird

The male Bower Bird who lives in Australia takes the top prize for home improvement. They attract a female by making the most spectacular nest possible. This bird builds a twig hut and decorates it with flowers, but he doesn't stop there. He will search for feathers, fruit, small pebbles or shells to decorate it. If near a city or town, he will add bits of glass, paper or string. His favourite thing to decorate with is blue objects like water bottle caps, pens or biros and anything else he can find that's the same colour he is.

This fancy nest can take months for a Bower Bird to build. They are very fussy about what their nest looks

A male Bee Hummingbird collects nectar from a firebush flower.

like and will make a lot of changes until they're satisfied. When he finally likes his nest creation, the Bower Bird will do a love dance, offering a gift of one of the nest decorations to his sweetie.

One type of Bower Bird does all this and more. He paints the walls of his nest mansion with his own blue or dark green spit!

How did bird brains get bigger?

Slowly, over many generations, animals change. The ones who are the best at finding food and shelter and defending themselves from their predators are the ones that survive. Their babies inherit (this means get from parents) the best abilities to live and have their own babies.

Barn Owls are night-time hunters. Even though they have very good eyesight, they can catch their prey just by listening for them.

To do this, creatures need to change their bodies and their brains. This is called adapting. To survive, we must all adapt to change and new challenges.

Humans, through our long history, have adapted to have bigger and better brains, to be taller and stronger and to be able to run fast.

Birds have also adapted, in different ways. Some got better and stronger wings, which means that they fly more than they run. Others gave up on flying to get paddle fins, like the penguins, who never fly except through the water, but are clumsy on land.

Today, as our climate gets warmer, some birds are changing their range. Range means all the places they live. Others are changing their migration patterns. That's where they spend the nesting season of the

A colourful Mandarin Duck. They live in Asia and also in California.

year, and where they go for the rest of the year. The travel in between is called migration.

Bird brains, like any creature's brain, get bigger to meet new needs, or new opportunities in their lives.

What can birds hear?

Most birds have much better eyesight than hearing. They only need to hear things that are close to them and might mean danger. Other things they need to hear, like the calls of their mates or their own kind are also usually close to where they are.

The bird with the best hearing is the Barn Owl. They can hear sounds that are 10 miles, or 16 kilometres away.

Even more astonishing, scientists have proven that Barn Owls can find a mouse that is under snow, at night when it's totally dark out and even when the Barn Owl has a blindfold covering its eyes. They do it by listening for the sound of the mouse's heartbeat. Barn Owls live almost everywhere in the world except where it is very cold and on some islands in the Pacific Ocean.

Can birds see in color?

When you look at sparrows or wrens, you might think, "well they're just sort of grayish and brownish. Pretty boring."

In fact, that 'boring' bird could be riot of colours more spectacular than any other bird you've ever seen. Here's why.

Humans have three colour cones in our eyes. We can see three colours (black and white too, but they don't count). The three colours are yellow, blue and red. You've probably seen these colours, called the colour wheel because all the colours humans can see are these three, or made from these three. For example, to get green you mix blue and yellow. Want orange? Mix red and yellow.

Birds have four colour cones in their eyes. They see red, blue, yellow and ultraviolet light, also called UV

This is a Bald Eagle. Bald Eagles live in Canada, United States and Mexico. They always live near a lake or the ocean.

light. They see in colour in ways we can only imagine. They know colors we have no names for.

Birds see many more colours in everything – leaves, flowers, their own feathers – than we can. We are almost colour-blind, compared to birds.

The birds with the best sight are the ones that are diurnal. This means normally awake during the day and asleep at night.

Bird Fun Fact:

In their lifetime, the average Albatross will fly more than 10 million miles, or more than 16 million kilometres. That's the same distance as going to the moon and back to Earth again 20 times!

The Kiwi Bird is about as big as a chicken and lives only in New Zealand. Its loose feathers are more like fur.

The night birds tend to be not so good at seeing colours, but better at seeing where there is low light, or almost no light.

Why birds see UV light

Why is being able to see UV light useful for birds?

Some food, like berries, reflect UV light. This makes the berries easier to see among the leaves, making berry eating easier.

Raptors like hawks and eagles hunt their small prey, like mice, not by seeing them. Instead, they fly above the fields hoping to spot mice pee splashes and pee trails because pee reflects UV light. Where there's pee

It's the Duck Patrol! These Mallard Ducks are all males. The females have brown heads.

there might be dinner even if no mouse or rat or vole is in sight.

Birds can easily tell the difference between males and females of their kind, even though humans often can't. The reason is they look very different with UV light vision. Birds use this to help them find mates, defend their territory and recognize other members of their flock.

Another way some birds use their UV vision power is to recognize their own eggs and eject an egg some other bird has left in their nest.

Birds in camo

Some birds have feathers that are so close in color to their habitat, or the place they live, that it is hard to even see them among the branches or leaves.

Birds use camo to protect themselves and their chicks. Some birds that do this are Mallard Ducks, Sparrows, Woodcocks, Whip-poor-wills and Sandpipers. Their super-power is blending in with their habitat.

Some birds, like male Cardinals and Goldfinches, are brilliantly coloured in mating season, but their colours get duller in other seasons of the year.

Young birds are usually wearing camo until they're adults, to protect them. Birds that live on the ground or mostly there are also the ones that usually have camo colours.

What can birds smell?

Most birds don't need to be able to smell water, or food, or dangerous predators. They only need their keen eyesight and hearing to help them do all these jobs.

But there are some exceptions. The Kiwi Bird, a night-time hunter, has such terrible eyesight they are almost blind. But they are brilliant at smelling things. They can stick the tip of their beaks in the ground and smell an earthworm, their favorite treat, that is 6 inches, or 15 centimetres, underground. Then they find a stick and dig around until they get their worm.

There are birds that can't fly, but only one can't fly because it has no wings. It's included in the bird family because, in every other way, it's a bird.

It's the Kiwi Bird. It's the only bird to have its nostrils on the end of its beak.

Bird Fun Fact:
Most birds fly at about 25 miles per hour, or 40 kilometres per hour.

How do birds sleep?

Birds can sleep standing up because they are able to lock their feet on a branch and lock their legs. Some birds use sleep to get through the coldest weather. They are able to slow their heartbeats, lock their feet, lower their own body temperature and doze for several days when they need to.

Some birds can sleep with one eye open. Half their brain is resting while the other half stays awake, watching out for danger. Birds that fly long distances can doze while they glide on air currents.

Flamingos, herons and egrets are all wading birds. They stand in water to sleep because the water protects them. They know if an enemy is getting close, they will feel the water moving and hear it making sounds to warn them. They can wake up quickly and escape.

Ducks and geese also use waterbeds, floating around and dozing on the water.

Many birds get together in flocks at night. This helps them all stay warm and safe.

Birds tuck their faces into their shoulders or backs when they're sleeping. They do this so they'll always be breathing in warm air.

Why is bird poop white?

Birds eat seeds and nuts that are brown, worms that are pinkish, berries that are red or purple, and other colorful foods. So why is their poop mostly white?

The Snowy Owl is also known in their home in the Far North as Ookpik, which means Ghost Owl.

Their pee and poop is mixed together. It is mostly white because there is a lot of uric acid turning it white. Uric acid is the parts of food that the body doesn't need, so it goes to the kidneys and then out of the body. Birds use this system because it keeps most of the water in their bodies. Mammals, including humans, have a completely different body system that uses more water to get the waste materials out of our bodies.

Birds evolved to not need as much water because water would add more weight to their bodies. Evolved means changes, over many thousands of years or longer. Birds needed to be as light as possible to be able to fly.

Raptors

Raptors are birds that hunt other birds and animals for food. Another name for them is Birds of Prey. All Eagles, Condors, Falcons, Hawks, Vultures, Buzzards, Secretary Birds and Owls are Birds of Prey.

They catch and kill their prey with their powerful feet.

Falcons have been given an important job at airports, where they help staff keep flocks of birds away from the planes and helicopters that are taking off and landing. The Raptors are sent out on patrols several times a day. They check around the hangars and along the airfields to make sure there are no seagulls or other birds that could hit the planes. Flocks of birds have hit planes in the air, causing damage to the engines.

The smallest Bird of Prey is the Falconlet. They're only about as big as a Sparrow. They live in southeast Asia.

Owls

Owls don't build their own nests. They look for the nests of other birds, or hollows in trees, or abandoned buildings to make their home.

Owls can fly in the rain, but if they get completely wet they won't be able to fly at all until their feathers are dry again. Their feathers don't have the same oily coating other birds' feathers have to make them waterproof. But they can be completely silent when they're flying, something no other type of birds can do.

Owls eat every part of the small animals they kill. They get rid of the parts they can't digest, like bones, fur and teeth, by throwing it up in a lump.

Do birds like to play?

If you've ever watched birds splashing in a puddle or swooping in the air, you might think that they're just playing and you'd be right! Birds like to play as much as people do.

Some crows at a university campus in Vancouver have learned how to mimic dogs barking. They wait until there are lots of people walking about between classes or at lunchtime. Then they fly low over the students barking the whole time.

The startled students scatter in alarm. The crows go back to their trees where they probably tell each other how much fun that was.

Young Peregrine Falcons play fight with their brothers and sisters. They take turns pretending to be the predator bird or the prey bird. They swoop out of the air, practicing their flying and hunting skills. It looks like playing, and it is, but they're also learning how to be successful adults.

Birds never sweat

Birds can't sweat. They have other ways to cool off in hot weather. They rest in the shade, or fly up higher to glide on air currents where it's cooler.

This is a Western Yellow Wagtail. They live in Britain in summer and migrate to Africa in winter.

Birds can also pant like a dog to cool off. They look for shallow water, like a birdbath, for a cooling dip.

Vultures poop on their own legs because the poop cools them as it dries. It's white, so it reflects light and heat. That's just like you wearing white clothes in summer to be cooler.

Some birds just don't like hot weather. They migrate to milder places for part of the year.

Bird Fun Fact:

There are 17 species of penguins in the world today. They all live south of the Equator in the Southern Hemisphere. The only penguins in the northern half of the world all live in zoos.

What is the dawn chorus?

The dawn chorus is the early morning concert songbirds present in Spring and Summer. It happens at sunrise, or just before.

But how do birds know what time to start singing?

They can sense only very small changes in light. When the light gets to a certain point at almost the end of night, they start to sing.

Of all songbirds, North American Robins are the earliest to start the dawn symphony. But they don't always get it right. The glow of streetlights can set a Robin singing long before the sun comes up!

There is also a dusk chorus at the end of day, but it is usually softer, with fewer birds joining in.

The smallest bird in the world

Bee hummingbirds are the world's smallest birds. They're also, for their size, the biggest eaters in the entire bird world.

Bee Hummingbirds are less than 3 inches or 7.6 centimetres long. Half of that is their long beak and their tail. They weigh just half an ounce, or 1.6 grams. That's about the same weight as just one pencil, or an empty soda pop can.

A bee hummingbird can beat its wings 80 times per second! During breeding season, even they break their own record for wing-beats, with their wings flapping at 200 beats per second!

Bee hummingbirds don't migrate, so to see them you will have to visit their home in the coastal forests of Cuba.

Do birds sing at night?

Some do, sometimes, but scientists aren't sure why. It could be because it's a quieter time, so it's easier to be heard!

Or it might be because of yard lights and streetlights, making the birds think it must be dawn.

The Willie Wagtail of Australia sings at night, but mostly when there's bright moonlight.

Alarm calls

Birds use their alarm calls to tell their mates there is a predator nearby. Alarm calls can warn the predator to stay away. Males also use alarm calls to let other males know to stay in their own territory.

Chicadees get their name for their call that sounds like Chicka – dee – dee – dee. The dees are alarm calls. The more dees there are, the more anxious the bird is.

Bird Fun Fact:

Bird scientists think there are somewhere between 100 billion and 400 billion birds alive today. 10 billion of them live in the US.

This is a Great Egret, also called a Heron. They use their knife-sharp bill to catch fish or small animals and eat them whole.

Big eaters!

Hummingbirds are always hungry. They spend almost all their awake time looking for food. Sometimes they eat insects, but mostly they eat flower nectar. A bee hummingbird can visit 1,500 flowers in a single day!

All hummingbirds have a very fast metabolism. They're living much faster than we are. Their hearts beat about 1,000 times per minute. Human hearts beat about 60 to 100 times a minute. How fast your body works is called metabolism [say this: met-tab-bow-lism]. Having a fast metabolism takes a LOT of energy, so they have to eat a lot of food.

The Kea of New Zealand is a mountain Parrot. They're a smart bird, able to make tools and work together to get food.

Can you guess how much food you'd have to eat in just one day, if you had the same metabolism as a hummingbird? The answer is you'd need to eat 300 cheeseburgers every single day to keep your body working as fast as a hummingbird's body works. Then you'd have to do a LOT of exercises and running around to use up all that food energy!

Some birds can fly backwards

Hummingbirds are the arial acrobat All-Stars of the bird world. They are the only birds that can hover and the only birds that can fly upside down. But hummers are not the only bird that can fly backwards.

Herons and egrets can do this trick, too. They usually only do it when they're fighting with another bird.

Warblers fly forwards, then backwards to catch the insects they eat.

Smart birds

There is only one mountain parrot in the world, that we know of. It's the Kea, a large parrot that lives only on the South Island of New Zealand.

They might also be the world's smartest bird. They are as intelligent as chimpanzees.

Can birds laugh?

There is no bird, or any other animal that laughs because they think something is funny. Only humans have the ability to do this.

However, there are birds who sound like they're laughing. Kookaburra birds, who live in Australia and New Guinea, are famous for their loud call that sounds like crazy loud laughing. There's even a song about it. Maybe you sang it at summer camp?

Birds that are good at repeating sounds they've heard can also mimic humans laughing. Parrots, crows and myna birds can make laughing sounds.

Seagulls are clever at stealing from people who aren't paying attention to their sandwich or chips.

Bird thieves!

If you're at the beach, hang onto your hotdog! Seagulls are watching you, and they're ready to dash in and grab a free lunch! Seagulls will also steal food from beach bags, tents and off picnic tables.

They can break into cottages and shoplift treats from convenience stores and market stalls.

Seagulls aren't the only bird thieves out there.

Blue Jays mostly eat seeds and nuts. They steal food from each other and hide it in caches. A cache is like a personal food pantry, hidden underground or under some rocks. Blue Jays also watch each other hiding food and steal from other Blue Jays' caches.

It's a myth that crows only steal shiny objects. Crows will steal anything they like or think they want. But crows can also be generous. They will leave gifts of the things they find for people they like.

More about Seagulls

It's easy to think of Seagulls as pest birds. They're messy, noisy and they all want to steal our lunch. But there are also some remarkable things about them. They mate for life and are good parents. They're excellent fliers. Some migrate for many thousands of miles or kilometres. For example, Seagulls who summer in Northern Scotland fly south to Africa to enjoy a warmer winter.

Seagulls are also clever birds. They stamp their feet to sound like rain beginning to fall to trick earthworms to come up to the surface, where hungry Seagulls are waiting to give the worms a big welcome! They also find mussels and drop them onto rocks to break them open. Then a Seagull can eat the soft creatures inside their hard shells. When this doesn't work, they drop mussels on roads and wait for a passing car to run over the mussel, crushing the shell.

That's a smart bird, using humans to get what they want!

Bird Fun Fact:
Emus, who look like a shorter version of Ostriches, have very strong leg muscles for running. They can go forwards, but cannot walk backwards, unlike almost every other land animal.

Toucans have big beaks that help them grab fruit from trees. They are a songbird, but their song sounds more like barking, growling or frogs croaking.

Mute Swans are big eaters. Each one can eat up to 8 pounds or 3.63 kilograms of lake-bottom grasses every day.

Strongest bird

It takes great strength to take off from the ground and fly. Some birds spend most of their lives in the air. Others fly for great distances each year, migrating to another country or even another continent. They stay there for several months, then make the return journey, back to almost exactly where they started.

The strongest birds take off and fly while carrying heavy burdens. One of these is the Bald Eagle. Bald Eagles have been spotted lifting a mule deer into the air and flying it back to their nests to feed their chicks. Mule deer weight about 15 pounds, or 6.8 kilograms.

Why do birds have beaks?

Birds have no teeth and no lips. Instead, they have a beak, or bill. Birds use their beaks to get food, groom themselves, build their nests and care for their chicks.

What bird has the most feathers?

How many feathers does a bird have? Would you answer 2,000? Or 5,000? Or 25,000?

All of these answers are correct. Small songbirds, like chickadees and sparrows, have between 1,500 and 3,000 feathers. Larger birds, like Eagles, have between 5,000 and 8,000 feathers. Swans are the birds with the most feathers. The Whistling Swan has 25,200 feathers.

Wondering what bird has the least feathers? It's the Ruby-Throated Hummingbird, with just 940 feathers.

Going for a big meal. Really big!

What meat-eating bird can capture, kill, carry away and eat the largest prey creature?

Raptors are known for their incredible strength in taking animals bigger than themselves. They can take off and fly carrying animals that weigh more than they do. Sometimes, a lot more.

Here are the birds that have been seen taking home a BIG load of dinner:

African Crowned Eagles prey on duikers, a small antelope that can weight as much as 75 pounds or 34 kilograms.

Philippine Eagle nests have been found with an entire deer skeleton in them. They've been seen carrying off adult monkeys and pythons.

Golden Eagles can carry a small Mountain Sheep or Mountain Goat off to their nests.

Harpy Eagles, who live in Peru, are called the world's most powerful bird of prey. They've been seen taking Howler Monkeys back to their nests.

What bird is the strangest eater?

Some birds are vegetarians. They only eat flower nectar or plant seeds or fruit like berries. Others are carnivores. This means they eat meat, like other birds' eggs or chicks, small creatures like mice or rats or even larger animals, like baby sheep or goats.

Then there are the truly strange eaters, like the Ostrich, who will eat, or try to eat, just about anything. Veterinarians trying to help an Ostrich with a stomach ache at the London Zoo in England found he'd swallowed an alarm clock, a roll of photography film, a handkerchief, a piece of rope, a bicycle valve, a pencil, three gloves, a small piece of jewellery and seven coins. It's a mystery how he managed to find all these things to eat, especially when zoo people give the animals all the healthy food they need.

An Ostrich mother and her very large family. An Ostrich can live for 75 years!

Ostrich

There's more that's odd about the world's largest living bird, the Ostrich.

Usually, animals that have large families don't live for very long. Animals that only have one or two babies at a time and don't have babies very often usually live a lot longer. This isn't true for Ostriches, who have large families AND long lives.

They have the longest stride of any bird when they're running, up to 23 feet or 7 metres! Stride means the distance between each step they take.

They run faster than any other bird, up to 45 miles per hour, or 72.5 kilometres per hour. That's just a bit

Ostriches are a social bird, and dangerous if you get too close. An Ostrich's kick is powerful enough to kill a lion.

faster than the fastest human can run.

They do their running on feet that have two toes.

They lay the largest eggs of any bird. One ostrich egg is as big as a ripe cantaloupe! That's about the same size as 24 chicken eggs put together.

Ostriches have the largest eyes of any animal that lives on land today. Ostrich eyes are two inches, or 5 centimetres, across. That's five times bigger than a human eye!

They are the tallest bird and also the heaviest, which is why they can't fly. An adult ostrich can be 9 feet, or 2.7 metres tall! They can weigh up to 345 pounds or 156 kilograms! That's one VERY big bird, big enough to attack and, very rarely, kill a person.

The Ural Owl lives In Scandinavia, throughout Europe and across Asia all the way to Japan. Couples sing duets when they're courting (that means dating).

Killer birds!

Birds that are capable of seriously hurting or killing people are Ostriches, Emus, Cassowaries (they live in Australia) and some owls such as Bearded Owls, Great Horned Owls and Barred Owls. Take care if you happen to meet any of these outlaw birds! They do attack when they feel threatened.

Birds that never fly

Ostriches aren't the only birds that never fly. Others are Emus, Cassowaries, Kiwi Birds and Penguins.

Canada Goose babies, called goslings, have to grow up fast. Just a few months from when they're this big, they'll need to migrate from their nesting homes in Canada to their winter vacations in Central and Southern United States.

Bird bones

In order to be able to fly, birds had to change their bones, from the heavy and almost solid bones of land reptiles like dinosaurs, to something that was still strong, but much lighter. These stronger, lighter bones also helped the land birds that can't fly run faster.

Wings like hands

Wings aren't just something like our hands. They are the same bones, made longer or shorter, for a new purpose. We use our hands to pick up and use things. Birds turned their hands into wings. Thumbs became a

If there was a contest for Ugly Bird, this Vulture might be a finalist!

grasping claw. Fingers grew longer, to support the wing feathers.

Hands first appeared in animals that live on land about 300 million years ago.

World's ugliest bird

Some birds are plain and even boring to look at. Some of them you might call ugly, like condors. Then there's the Marabou Stork of South Africa, a bird that is even uglier than ugly. Some people say this large bird looks like a bird vampire, only with a bald pink head. They like to live close to people's garbage, at landfill sites or dumps.

The Shoebill is related to pelicans and herons. The chicks call out to their parents to beg for food using a sound that is just like a human with the hiccups.

Look past all this and this large bird is amazing. It has a big body, but it can fly. Its massive wings are 3.7 metres, or more than 12 feet wide from wing-tip to wing-tip, when they're in the air.

Like vultures, Marabou Storks like to eat dead animals. Marabou Storks are so fierce, they often steal their food from the vultures.

The bird with a shoe on its face

If you visit Sudan or Zambia in Africa, you might see a rare Shoebill. This odd bird got their name because they look like they have a big shoe attached to their face. That's their bill, or beak. Not only is it big, it has sharp edges, helping Shoebills hunt for and crush snakes, lizards and rats.

Poison birds

There are plenty of animals that use poisons to protect themselves or stun their prey, but did you know that some of these are birds?

There is no bird that scientists have discovered that makes venom, like some snakes do. No bird can inject venom, like a mosquito can. The way that some birds can be poison to other creatures or people is they pick up poisons from plants or insects they eat. This poison is stored in their skin or their feathers. If it is a bird that people touch, or a type of bird some people eat, the people can get sick.

There are only five types of birds that can be poisonous. None of these poison-carrying birds lives in United States or Canada. Only one lives in Europe. It is the Common Quail and it's only poisonous during the time of year when they are migrating. Even though it is well known that Common Quails eat poisonous plants and so the Quails can be poisonous for people to eat, Quail is a popular food in Europe.

The real mystery is how some birds can eat poisonous things and not get sick or die themselves. Instead, their bodies are able to store the poison and then use it to defend themselves!

Why don't they get zapped?

To understand why birds on wires don't get zapped – or hardly ever – first you need to know something about electricity and how it works.

Electricity is lazy. It's always trying to find the shortest, easiest way to get back down to the ground. Anything that can form a pathway is called a conductor of electricity. That means it's the easy way for the electricity to travel. Metal, wood and water are all conductors. Since the bodies of animals, and also humans, are mostly made of water, we are also good conductors.

When birds are on wires, they are sitting on top of the wires. They don't give the electricity anywhere to go, or any easy path to the ground. When a bird, or any other creature, makes a bridge between two wires or connectors, the electricity might find that path to the ground. The result is the connector gets zapped.

A male Turkey. Turkeys first appeared in North America 20 million years ago.

The only way to stop the connection would be with an insulator. Insulators do not allow electricity to travel through them. Some insulators are rubber, glass, oil, very dry wood, air and diamonds.

What bird lives the longest?

Most wild birds have short lives, compared to how long most people live. With good care, pet birds usually live longer than their wild cousins. Generally, larger birds live longer than the smallest ones.

Birds that live high up in the trees live longer than ones that live and nest on the ground. Birds that live on islands tend to live longer than birds that live in cities.

The small owls have much shorter lives than the larger types of owls.

Ruby-throated hummingbirds look tiny and delicate, but they can live to age 9. Turkeys can only live up to 15 years, but a Great Horned Owl can get to be 30 years old. Twenty-seven is elderly for a Mallard Duck, but not for a Flamingo, who can live to be almost 50. There is a Laysan Albatross who is 68. She is the oldest living wild bird that scientists know about. But even 68 is still young, compared to some pet Parrots. There are many stories of Parrots living to be 100 years old, and more.

Flamingos

What would you think if eating a certain food made you turn color? And then you'd stay that way. Would it be odd? Or really cool?

That's what happens with flamingos. They aren't really pink. They turn pink or get even pinker when they eat blue-green algae and shrimp. The reason is there is a nutrient (that means healthy stuff) in this food called carotenoids [say this: care-oh-tin-oyds].

There are carotenoids in human foods, too, such as fruits or vegetables that are orange. Human bodies use carotenoids to help us not get sick. Plants use carotenoids to protect them from getting burnt by the sun. Birds that eat plants with carotenoids have red, orange or yellow feathers.

Flamingos can twist their necks. A group of Flamingos is called a flamboyance of Flamingos.

Some female birds choose their mates for their brilliant colors. To them, a male with bright dark colors means he's healthy and attractive. But we know it also means that bird has eaten plenty of carotenoids and that's what makes him so healthy. Birds also think that a healthy mate will be better at finding food.

This is likely also true for the flamingos, though they turn pink, rather than the red of Cardinals or the yellow of Goldfinches.

More about Flamingos

Flamingos have black feathers under their wings. You can only see their black feathers when they're flying.

Grey-Crowned Cranes are an elegant bird that lives in Eastern and Southern Africa.

Baby flamingos are grey. They only turn pink when they become adults at two years old.

In some places, flamingos are pale pink or even white. It all depends on what they eat.

Highest flier

If you took a ride on an airplane, could you look out the window and see birds flying past the window?

To answer this question, first you need to know how high up in the air you are when you're in an airplane. Passenger planes normally cruise at between 31,000 and 38,000 feet (or 9,448 metres to 11,582 metres) above earth. This is the same as being almost 6 miles to just a bit more than 7 miles (or 9.6 to 11.2 kilometres) up in the air!

Can a bird really fly that high? Yes, some can. A Ruppel's Vulture actually hit a plane back in 1973. At the time, the plane was cruising at 37,000 feet. The plane landed safely, but with a damaged engine.

Irish Air Control tracked 30 Whooper Swans at the almost cruising height of 27,000 feet in 1967. They were migrating from Iceland to Loch Foyle, near the border between Northern Ireland and Republic of Ireland.

Common Cranes are also high-fliers. They live in Northern Europe and parts of Asia. Some of them fly over the world's highest mountains, the Himalayas.

There is much less oxygen in the air this far above earth. These birds have adapted in amazing ways to be able to fly where there is too little oxygen for humans to survive. The highest we can go, without needing an oxygen mask, is 20,000 feet or 6,100 metres above earth.

Chickens

Chickens are familiar to most people because we often see them on a plate. It's easy to think of them as just food and not a bird.

Chickens are the most popular bird on earth. There are more chickens than any other type of bird.

A rooster Chicken with his girls, the hens. Like many animals and some birds, Chickens each have their own personality. Some people have Chickens as pets.

The males are called roosters and females are hens. Hens can crow, but roosters crow louder and more often. They use crowing to announce their own territory (that's their home and their own yard) to other roosters, telling them to stay away. They also use crowing as a call about danger to the hens and chicks.

Rooster crowing contests are a popular sport in several countries, including United States.

Sometimes two hens try to share a nest of eggs and both sit on it at the same time. When this doesn't work out (it usually doesn't) they will try to sit on top of each other, or there will be a hen-fight. Hens also sometimes steal the eggs of other hens and hatch them as their own.

What is an ornithologist?

A person who is a trained expert in birds is called an ornithologist [say this Orr-ni-tholl-oh-jist]. It is their job to study birds. People who have a hobby of being interested in birds are called birders or birdwatchers. Another name for them in Britain is twitchers.

Pigeons

There are about 260 million pigeons in the world, making them a very successful bird. While you might think they're just a pest (many people who live in cities do think this), pigeons are amazing fliers.

They can take off like a helicopter and fly straight up in the sky to a height of 20 metres, or 65 feet. That's about as high as a six-storey building!

They do it by first crouching, then use their powerful knees to leap straight up into the air while flapping their wings. Pigeons can accelerate from a standing start to flying at 60 miles per hour or 100 kilometres per hour in less than two seconds!

Pigeons aren't just fast at getting off the ground. They can fly up to 100 kilometres per hour (or 60 miles per hour). A pigeon can easily fly 800 kilometres, or 500 miles in a day!

This is a Victoria Crowned Pigeon. They live only in New Guinea. Do you think their spectacular crowns might have given people the idea for fascinator hats?

Pigeons also have incredible eyesight. They can see things that are up to 10 miles, or 16 kilometres away.

Hero birds

There are plenty of stories of heroic deeds done by dogs, horses and even cats who rescued people, but what about birds? Are there any Bird Heros?

The answer is YES. Miners used to take canaries down the pit with them, because the birds would faint if dangerous gasses were in the air. This warned the miners to grab the canary cages and get back up to the surface in a hurry, before they were poisoned. In this way, the canaries saved many lives.

During World War I, 1914 to 1918, pheasants could hear the buzz of enemy aircraft long before the soldiers did. The shrieks of the pheasants sounded the alarm to take cover, saving more human lives.

In World War II, 1939 to 1945, carrier pigeons carried messages. At times, the pigeons were the only way there was to send messages from and to soldiers on the battlefields. Pigeons often flew from behind enemy lines or to find downed planes at sea. They were trained to ride in the underbelly of rescue planes and peck on a button when they spotted crews clinging to downed planes or on life rafts. Many people did not die because pigeons went for help or spotted them from a plane so they could be rescued.

In the American Army, all warrior pigeons held the rank of Captain. Soldier pigeons carried life-saving messages across jungles, deserts and the Arctic.

In World War II, messenger pigeons were hunted down by Hitler's Platoon of Falcons. Many Wartime Pigeons arrived to deliver messages badly wounded and many died. 32 pigeons were honoured by Britain as heros of that war. They were presented with the Dickins Medal, also called the Animals' Victoria Cross, for gallantry. They represent the many thousands of brave birds who helped people survive these wars.

In 2017, the French military began training Golden Eagles to intercept suspicious or enemy drones scoping out military sites. Police in Holland also use trained eagles to catch drones.

There are many stories of pet Parrots saving members of their families. Here is one. One day Willie the Parrot started screaming loudly and flapping his wings. His owner thought this was odd, but didn't do anything. So Willie stared shouting "Mama baby" over and over. The owner went to check on her little daughter, age 2, who was playing in another room. She was choking and already turning blue. The owner knew what to do and soon her daughter was breathing normally again. Willie, Bird Hero, received an Animal Lifesaver Award from the Red Cross.

Loon

Loons are known for their eerie laugh. A shy bird, they are fiercely protective of their chicks. They will attack anyone, including humans, who comes too close to their babies.

Every loon can hold their breath long enough to stay underwater for five minutes without needing to come

Loons have red eyes. The males and females look the same. This is unusual in the bird world, where males are usually more colourful than females.

up for air. Some loons can stay underwater for much longer – as long as 15 minutes. Most people can stay underwater for half a minute, or a little more. The human record is 24 minutes underwater, without a new breath of air.

Woodcock

Woodcocks have upside-down brains. The part of their brain that controls walking, flying and other moving around is called the cerebellum [ser-re-bell-um]. A Woodcock's cerebellum isn't at the back of their skull, like it is with most animals. Instead, it's underneath the rest of their brain.

Another odd thing about Woodcocks is that their ears aren't further back on their head. Instead, their ear openings are right under their eyes!

Are the birds talking about you?

Some of them could be. North American Robins are able to recognize people by how they walk and what times of day they are usually outside. It could be the Robins are looking for other signals. They might be able to recognize human faces.

Pigeons and Crows can do all these things, and so can pet Parrots. They also remember people, especially the ones they don't like. AND they tell their friends all about who they don't like and why. Crow parents even teach their chicks who to like and who to not like, or sometimes even attack.

It seems that some birds are talking about the humans. Let's hope what they're saying about you is good.

Colored birds

Birds use color in many ways. One way is color helps them recognize each other. Some types of birds have brighter colors only in mating season. Males use their bright colors to attract a healthy female.

A male Peacock. Only the males have their spectacular coloured feathers.

For other birds, color is a disguise. They want to blend in with where they live, making it harder for their enemies to see them.

Really slow birds

Birds have a higher metabolism than we do. Their bodies are warmer than ours are and their hearts beat faster. But this doesn't always mean they do everything they do faster than humans can.

The bird with the slowest wing beats is the Vulture. It can stay in the air even when it flaps its wings only one time per second. Condors, pelicans and albatrosses are also slow flappers.

Pelicans are known for their big bills. They can hold three times as much food and water in their bills as their stomachs could hold.

The slowest flier is the Woodcock. They have been timed at just 5 miles per hour, or 8 kilometres per hour when they are doing their courtship flights. That's slower than most people can walk!

The slowest nest-builder in North America is the Baltimore Oriole. They can take 15 days to create a nest.

Long haul fliers

Many birds fly great distances to find food, the best nesting places and safety. By banding birds and tracking them, we can find out about some of these amazing journeys.

A Common Tern, a little shorebird, was banded in June, 1996, in Finland. It turned up on Rotamah Island in Australia seven months later. To do this epic journey of 16,250 miles, or 26,152 kilometres, it had to fly 125 miles or 201 kilometres a day, every day.

How do birds protect themselves from enemies?

Birds have found many ways to defeat their enemies. Different types of birds have different strategies. A strategy is a plan of action.

Some gather in flocks, with some birds always staying awake at night to be the flock's bodyguards. Some shelter in trees, abandoned buildings or even tunnel into the snow. Songbirds sing to announce their territory and scare off competitors.

The ones that don't fly have become fast runners. Or skilled swimmers and divers. Flying or running better or faster and finding good hiding places help birds dodge their enemies.

Birds that can be pets

Some birds can be friendly, coming to feeders and even landing in your hand to get seeds. But most birds do not make good pets. They would rather be wild animals.

Two small birds that can be happy as pets are both songbirds. They are Finches and Canaries. Keeping pet

Budgerigars, or Budgies, are a small parrot that are a popular pet.

Pigeons is a popular hobby, especially in England. There are also several types of Parrots that can be pets, including budgerigars or budgies, the smallest parrot.

Budgies and Canaries are fairly easy pets to have. All the other Parrots need more time and attention. They can be good pets, but not for beginner pet owners.

Of all the Parrots that can be pets, the African Grey is the best talker. They can hear a word or short sentence just once and then repeat it for the rest of their lives. Not only can they do this incredible remembering trick, but they will say that word or sentence and sound exactly like the person they heard saying it. They are brilliant mimics!

Birds with jobs

Birds do many jobs for people. One of them is helping the Yeo people in Africa hunt for honey. For hundreds of years, and perhaps longer, these people and Honey Guide Birds have worked together to find hidden beehives.

It is only recently that scientists have studied how this works. Astonishingly, they discovered that the people and the birds are talking to each other and understanding each other!

Many pet owners can communicate with their pets. But it is very rare for people and wild animals to be able to have a conversation! No one has ever trained the Honey Guide Birds to talk to people and work with people to get honey. They just learned to do it and

Spoonbill Cranes live everywhere except in Antarctica.

teach their chicks how to do it. Honey Guide Birds love the wax combs in bee hives, but they can't crack them open. That's the humans' job. The humans also smoke out the hives, protecting the birds from angry bee stings. Then the humans get the honey and leave the wax combs for a major bird feast!

More ways birds help people

Birds are beautiful, strange, smart and interesting. There are many ways they help people. If there were no birds, the world would be less beautiful and less magical. It might even be true that humans could not survive in a world without birds.

Birds help feed humans in many ways. There are the birds that we eat, including Chickens, Turkeys, Ducks, Geese, Partridge, Quail and some others. Birds also scatter the seeds of many plants, including trees. They help these plants find new places to grow. Some of these plants and trees give humans as well as other animals food or shelter, such as apple trees.

Birds are used for pest control for many food crops, such as coffee and grapes. They also pollinate many plants, just as bees, butterflies and many other types of insects do. We use seabird poop to make fertilizer to feed the plants that produce food.

Vultures, ravens and other scavenger birds are the clean-up crew for road kill.

Birds attract tourists in many places, creating needed jobs for people in the tourism and hospitality industries.

Birds we no longer have

Many animals are endangered. This means there aren't very many left in the world. Sometimes that's not enough for their species to go on. Every year, many species become extinct. Some of them are birds. Right now, more than 1,000 types of birds are endangered. That means they're dying out.

Once, almost everywhere in North America, there were huge flocks of Passenger Pigeons. Some people said there were so many that the skies would darken when a flock was flying by. It could take several minutes for just one flock to pass overhead. Then the settlers from Europe began to shoot at the Passenger Pigeons, killing them for target practice. They killed so

Once, the skies above United States and Canada were crowded with flocks of Passenger Pigeons. Now they are extinct.

many that the birds became endangered. The very last one died in a cage at Cincinnati Zoo in 1914.

Invasive species are plants or animals that don't belong. When they are brought to a different place than their home, they compete with the creatures that already live there. Sometimes, the newcomers are able to take all the food, so the natives die.

That's what happened to the Dodo, a bird that lived in Mauritius, an island in the Indian Ocean. They were larger than a turkey with a big head and blue-gray feathers. They were hunted by people and also attacked by new predators brought to the island by European explorers. The very last Dodo died in 1681.

We can never know about any special things about them, because they're gone.

Today, there are birds facing the same sad fate. Some birds that are very endangered in North America are California Condor, Mississippi Sandhill Crane and Ivory-billed Woodpecker. More than 200 birds are very endangered in Australia, including many types of Parrots and songbirds.

The good news is some people are working to save the birds. There are some birds that have been saved. Back in 1996, there were only 15 wild and 10 pet San Clemente Loggerhead Shrikes left in the world.

All of them lived on just one small island in California. Today, the goats and feral cats that attacked the birds are gone. Hundreds of birds that are the babies of the 10 pet birds have been released to be wild birds again. Their species has been saved.

Whooping Cranes are another bird that has come back from the edge of being extinct in North America. There were only 15 left in 1941. Today, there are three flocks, including the largest. It spends summers in Wood Buffalo Park in Alberta, Canada and winters at Aransas National Wildlife Refuge in Texas, United States. There are about 800 Whooping Cranes in North America now because humans saved them.

Another good news story is about Orange-bellied Parrots. Not long ago there were only 62 left in Australia. Today, they survive and their numbers are increasing.

Save the birds!

Many bird species are struggling. They've lost good places to live and find food. They've got some new enemies, like climate change and pollution. It's up to us to help them!

Ornithologists and other scientists say that nearly 1 of every 7 species of birds in the world today are at high risk. There are many ways you can join people worldwide who are working to save the birds!

1. Make nesting boxes. Smaller ones are places for birds to shelter and also build nests. Larger ones are good for owls. Look online for building plans. There are also good how-to videos on YouTube.

2. If you have a pet cat and you let them outside, put a bell on their collar so the ringing will warn the songbirds. Cats are fast and ferocious bird killers! Also, you will need to change the bell

often. Cats are smart. They learn how to move so the bell doesn't make any warning sounds. You can also use a bright-coloured collar on your cat to warn birds. There are sonar collars for cats that send warning sounds we can't hear to the birds. If you only let your cat out after dark, the birds will be safer, asleep in trees and other shelters where cats can't find them.

Cover windows. Birds don't understand what glass is and they will fly into windows, thinking it's just air. Putting a picture of a Falcon or Hawk in your window doesn't work. Birds don't see that as a real threat because it doesn't look like a Falcon or a Hawk the way they see them.

3. If a bird does hit your window, it will be stunned. Gently pick it up with gloves on. Put it in a quiet, dark, safe place to recover, like a shoebox with a cover and airholes punched in it. After an hour or so the stunned bird will try to flutter. That's when it's ready to be released and fly away. If it can't fly by then, take it to your local wildlife rescue centre.

4. If you find a baby bird and know where the nest is, put the baby back in her nest. If you don't know where the nest is, put the baby in a small basket or flowerpot with some leaves and dry grass in it. Put the basket or flowerpot close to where you found the baby bird.

5. Feed birds seeds, suet and slices of fresh oranges. Give them clean, fresh water. Put out sugar nectar for hummingbirds. Especially in the

month before migration, travelling birds need to fatten up for their long journeys.

6. Provide cool shelter for birds in very hot or very cold weather.

7. Plant bird-friendly shrubs and trees such as evergreens.

8. Plant bird-friendly and insect-friendly gardens to feed the birds.

9. Work with your friends to change or strengthen the laws that protect birds.

There are many ways you can make our world a better place by helping the birds. Now you know more about just how special they are in so many ways, I hope you will join bird lovers everywhere in helping the birds survive!

Thanks for reading!

Jacquelyn

Bird Fun Fact:

There are only three types of birds that aren't protected by any laws in United States. The reason is these three birds are very successful. They are the European Starling, Pigeon and Common or House Sparrow. All these birds are thriving.

About the Author

Jacquelyn Elnor Johnson started telling stories to entertain her younger sisters when she was 10. They were a tough audience! By age 15, she was a writing for the local newspaper and had written her first book. She went on to have careers in writing for and editing newspapers and magazines and teaching journalism in United States and Canada.

In 2014, she moved with her family to Nova Scotia, drawn by the opportunity to live near the ocean. A life-long pet lover, she is the bestselling author of 13 books about caring for and enjoying pets and animals, including **I Want A Bearded Dragon** and **The Complete Bearded Dragon Care Book**.

She also writes novels including the Morley Stories series for girls ages 10 to 13.

Find all her books and more at **www.CrimsonHillBooks.com**

PHOTO CREDITS

Thank you to these photo artists:

<u>Shutterstock</u>: Dotted Yeti, Fernando Calmon, Peter Kraayvanger, Ken Griffiths, Wang LiQiang, Vee Snijders, Jim Cumming, Martin Mecnarowski, John Navajo, Nataliya Hora and Panaiotidi

<u>Pixabay</u>: Simon Marlow, Kevins Photos, S. Hermann and F. Richter, Siggy Nowak, Gerhard G., J. Martizo, Congerdesign, Danny Moore, Sven Lachmann, Engin Akyurt, Edgar Calderon, Psubraty, Pavan Prasad, Barbara Fraatz, Tracey O'Brien, Ralphs Photos, Couleur, Klimkin, Photo-Rabe, Doug Smith, Alan Lau, James DeMers, Katja, Efraim Stochter, Rebecca Tregear, Coco Parisienne, Frank Winkler, Hans Braxmeier, Peter H., James DeMers, Nicky Pe and Erik Karits.

Loved all these bird facts? Discover MORE Fun Facts books from Crimson Hill Books:

- **Fun Dog Facts for Kids**
- **Fun Cat Facts for Kids**
- **Fun Leopard Gecko and Bearded Dragon Facts for Kids**
- **Fun Reptile Facts for Kids; Lizards, Turtles, Crocodilians, Snakes and Birds**
- **Fun Pony Facts for Kids**
- **Fun Horse Facts for Kids**
- **Fun Bird Facts for Kids**
- **Fun Backyard Bird Facts for Kids**
- **Fun Insect Facts for Kids**

And Don't Miss:

- **Dinosaur Facts for Kids**
- **T-rex Facts for Kids**